On the day before Christmas,
A Cowboy, homebound,

Rode into the desert
On a horse he called Brown.

He had long ago left
His family behind,

As he searched for their fortune
In an old desert mine.

Now the gold in his pocket
Felt more like a stone,

As he read his son's letter,
"Daddy, please come on home."

The Cowboy had promised
He'd be back Christmas Day,

But the snow in the mountains
Now stood in his way.

Coyote Christmas

A STORY BY TOM G. ROBERTSON
ORIGINAL ART BY JOHN RUNNE

Great American Opportunities Inc.
Publishers
Nashville, Tennessee

Coyote Christmas
Published by Great American Opportunities Inc.
Story by Tom G. Robertson
Illustrations by John Runne

Library of Congress Catalog Card Number:
93-072377
ISBN: 0-87197-800-8

Manufactured in the United States of America

First Printing: 1993   45,000 copies

The original art in this book was painted in acrylic on canvas.
The text type was set in Clearface Regular.
The display type was set in Bordeaux Roman and Viking Regular.
Color Separations by Color Systems.

Book Design by The Burgundy Group, Inc.

The dust devils swirled
And the sand stung his face

Beneath the great spires
That rose in this place.

The cold came on sudden
In the still desert air;

The Cowboy wished for home,
Instead of being out there.

As the last rays of sunlight
Played out on the spire,

He tied up old Brown
And made a tumbleweed fire.

He wrapped up in a blanket
To keep out the chill.

The horse gave a sh-shudder,
And the night grew still.

"Merry Christmas," he said softly
To the horse he called Brown,

And the Cowboy dozed off
Asleep on the ground.

He dreamed of the family,
That he held so dear,

And feared he'd not see them
At Christmas this year.

Old Brown flopped his eyelids
And wheezled a snore,

As he slept like the Cowboy
For a moment or more.

And then! All of a sudden!
A great howling came!

The Cowboy jumped up,
For the desert had changed.

The moon had risen
In the Eastern sky,

And the desert howled
With a Coyote cry.

The Coyotes skated and skied.
They sledded and slipped.

They had a belly giggle
As one of them flipped.

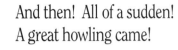

The Coyotes sang
And the Coyotes danced,

And the Coyotes pranced
'Round in cowboy pants!

And the Cowboy wondered,
"Could it possibly be

That at Christmastime here,
Coyotes dress just like me?"

They all wore tall hats
And boots and spurs,

And bright native dresses
For the Coyote girls.

A Coyote named Indy
Rolled on along,

As another named Belle
Sang a Coyote song.

A fiddler played loud
And howled at the moon,

And the Coyotes sang carols
Almost in tune.

They all looked so funny
That they tickled old Brown,

And he snortled horse giggles
With a whinnysnicker sound.

And after the music,
The time became right

To decorate the cactus
With bright Christmas light.

Up on the slopes
coyotes whizzed by

Patroling the Mesa,
Scanning the sky.

The Ski patrol searched,
Looking all through the night

Then howled "Hooray!"
Santa Paws was in sight.

And a Coyote Santa
Dressed in red and white

Whizzed down from the Mesa
Holding his light.

And to the children he gave
Coyote presents galore—

Bright colored rocks,
Cactus candy, and more.

For the Coyote boys,
There were lassos and spurs,

With cornhusk dolls
For the Coyote girls.

And a Coyote chieftain
In a feathered headdress

Had a howl of a chuckle
As he watched the night fest.

And three wise Coyotes
In their pink Cadillac

Spotted a star
And followed it back.

Then suddenly at midnight,
From that same star above,

Born upon the wind,
Came a brilliant light of love.

Its glow fell on the mission,
And many angels sang.

All the world was silent
As bells in whisper rang.

And Coyote howls turned
Into quiet song,

As one by one to the mission,
They all walked along.

And in their paws each carried
One small thing,

A simple gift of love
For the newborn King.

A piece of cactus, a flower,
A paw full of sand,

Treasure measured in the heart,
Taken from the land.

The Cowboy kept thinking
"What can I do?"

So he followed the Coyotes
Into the mission, too.

A wise Coyote preacher
Howled a Coyote "Howl-o!"

And said, "Welcome my friend,
With your chunk of gold.

Does the gold own you
As others I have known?

And is gold the reason
That you're not at home?"

The cowboy reached for the gold
And laid the piece down

Gave his gift and turned
To the horse he called Brown.

As he left the mission
On that joyous desert night,

All the heavens and the earth
Filled with a wondrous light.

And the mission bells tolled
"Let there be Peace on Earth"

On this night of nights,
Upon the Christ Child's birth.

When he woke in the morning,
There was not a sound.

No sign at all
Of the strange Coyote town.

Just the same old desert,
How funny it seemed.

Did it really happen,
Or was it only a dream?

Then it occurred to the Cowboy
That there might still be time

To make good his promise
At this Christmastime.

He jumped on old Brown
Who reared up to the sky

And ran like the wind—
He could almost fly!

The Cowboy didn't notice
The gold on the ground.

It meant nothing now,
As they raced homeward bound!

They crossed the wide prairie
Toward a small distant light,

Through Rabbit Ears Pass,
They'd be home tonight!

It was just before midnight
When they made it home.

Thank goodness, this Christmas
They would not be alone.

The Cowboy's little boy
Heard an old familiar knock

And that whinneysnicker sound
As he undid the lock.

He opened the door wide,
And called out to his mom

Through laughter and through tears,
"Daddy's come home!"

All about the Coyotes,
The Cowboy explained,

And what he had seen,
How little he'd gained.

They laughed at his "howling"
Just like Coyotes do,

And the spirit of Christmas
Inside of them grew!

The boy asked his daddy
If someday he could see

The mysterious Coyotes
And their families.

The Cowboy reached down
And picked up his son

And smiled as he answered
And remembered the fun.

"But never go at Christmas
And never for the gold"

For Christmas is for family
When we need someone to hold.

And from far far away
A howl said Amen.

And old Brown whinneysnickered
They were all home again!